DON'T BE OFFENDED.
THIS IS FOR ME TOO

ENCOURAGE

ELEVATE

Don't Be Offended.

This is for Me Too

For Encouragement

Mary L Lumsden

ENLIGHTEN

Xulon Press

Xulon Press

2301 Lucien Way #415
Maitland, FL 32751
407.339.4217
www.xulonpress.com

Unless otherwise indicated, Scripture
quotations taken from the King James Version
(KJV)–*public domain.*

Printed in the United States of America.

ISBN-13: 978-1-54565-700-3

FAITH

F - avor of God

A - ssurance from God

I - nterest in God

T - houghts of God

H - ealing from God

You get the Favor of God when you believe God, then He gives you Assurance that He's with you. Because you have taken Interest in Him by reading

His words, now you have His Thoughts in your mind and heart. He can begin Healing you in every area of your life.

Mary L. Lumsden

DON'T FEEL OFFENDED:
THIS IS FOR ME, TOO,
BECAUSE WHO AM I TO
NOT ACCEPT THE TRUTH.
For Encouragement

MARY L. LUMSDEN

CONTENTS

THERE'S NO SUCH THING AS LUCK

There's no such thing as luck.

It is the Lord shedding His grace.

There's no such thing as luck to run this race.

In order to continue to receive His grace,

Don't take too long to get in place.

For surely one day you will have to meet

Him face to face.

DON'T GET COMFORTABLE

Don't get comfortable in this world;

Be comforted by JESUS in this world.

TORE UP, THEN FIXED UP

Matthew 26:53, John 17:19-21, Luke 22:32

The world will tear you up.

Then JESUS will show up.

Then the Lord has to pick

you up.

Then He will fix you up;

And then grow you up in

Christ Jesus.

LET GO

Isaiah 35:1-10, Hebrews 4:16

Let go of the pain,

And focus on the gain.

That is in Christ Jesus

you will obtain.

STOP RUNNING

2 Timothy 4:1-3, 5:15

Stop running from the life-saver (Jesus)

And running to the life-taker (Satan).

SURVIVAL IN THESE TIMES

For such a time as this, the heart of survival is wisdom. So read, study, know, and believe your Bible, because it is the Word of God that will help you to survive in this world.

DON'T THINK, ASK

Matthew 7:7-10, Deuteronomy 29:29

All thoughts come from not knowing. So, if you want to know, ask the One who knows it all, Jesus.

If He wants you to know, He will answer. If not, it wasn't for you to know.

POSSESSIONS

KJV-NLT 1 John 5:21, KJV Mark 10:17-23

We are more upset about Jesus getting rid of our possessions than what is possessing us. Remember your possessions should not be your obsessions.

THANK YOU, LORD

Thank you, Lord, for calming us down.

Thank you, Lord, for bringing us around.

Thank you, Lord, for shedding Your grace.

While we attempt to run this race,

You're always there when we call

To pick us up when we fall.

You place our feet on solid ground

And let us know you're always around.

Thank you, Lord, for who You are.

Thank for being my shining star.

Thank you for taking me under wing.

Thank you, Lord; You're my everything.

GET UP

Lord, help the men to stand up, not wimp up;

But wash up with the Blood of Jesus.

Then they can start up the call up on their lives

In Jesus Christ.

THE WRONG BOOK

KJV 1 Timothy 4:1-5, NLT. 2 Thessalonians 2:2-5

Looks like everybody's leaving the church.

They're going to Facebook;

But they're putting their faces in the wrong book.

There's coming a time when they're going to face

The creator of the true, holy Bible book.

Then how are you going to look?

Do not be sad; just be glad that you got caught

Before you really got hooked on that Facebook.

So let's not get hooked on this Facebook,

And forget the truth of the holy **Bible book.**

STRAIGHTEN
OR TAKEN OUT

John 10: 9-10

Jesus comes to straighten you out.

The devil comes to take you out.

Would you rather be straightened out?

Or would you rather be taken out?

THANK YOU, JESUS

I thank You, Jesus.

I thank You every day.

I thank You, JESUS.

I thank You in every way.

GET SELF OUT OF THE WAY

Put self on the shelf and God on the table,

Because He is the only one that is able.

He will pick you up when you fall.

He is the God that does it all.

He will dry all your tears,

And take away all your fears.

Then restore those lost years

When you could not hear

The call of God in your ear.

RESPECT YOURSELF
AND YOUR BODY

1 Corinthians 6:18-20, Leviticus 20:7-8

The body is a beauty to behold,

But should only be exposed

To your husband or wife I was told.

So don't give it to the world to exploit,

As if it is some kind of a sport.

Take pride in it and cover it up,

So you won't be treated like an open port.

THE WORLD'S VIEW

2 Timothy 3:2-7, NLT/KJV

I am so into me that I can't see You,

And I don t care what You say or do.

It's all about me and none of You.

So leave me alone and do what You do.

STOP LOOKING AT EVERYBODY ELSE

Matthew 7:1-5, Luke 6:37-42

Take your eyes off everybody else.

Take a look at yourself.

See what you can do to improve you, so that you can help someone else that doesn't feel so good about him/herself.

Let's not forget about Jesus, who created us to be a portrait of Himself; who died on the cross for you and for me.

LISTENING

James 1:19, Matthew 7:24, NIV Luke 11:28, James 1:22

If we're listening more than we're looking and talking, we can learn a lot of what Jesus is trying to teach us;

that is to take on His character.

MIND BATTLE

Romans 7:19, 24-25

Keep the Word of God in your mind. It will keep the devil out.

God deals with the heart; the devil battles for your mind.

Let God have your mind.

He will have your heart, also.

YOU ARE NOT IN CONTROL

Isaiah 45: 6-7 Proverbs 16: 9

It is hard to change from who we are, because we are so used to being who we want to be when GOD is calling us to be who He made us to be. So, we think that we are in control, but that is not true. Just look up. There's someone greater than you.

JESUS WILL
SHOW UP

KJV Luke 8:26-36

Jesus shows up, shows out, and show us that He is God and that He is real.

AT YOUR PACE

Lord, I was a sinner saved by Your grace.

As a child of God, I must this race

If I start slacking in my pace,

Please help me to stay in place.

One day, I will meet You face to face.

I will not complain; I will not haste,

Because the best results is at Your pace

While You continue to shed Your grace.

IT'S NOT ABOUT YOU

John 3:16-18 Mark 16:15-18

Stop looking at yourself and do what Jesus does.

Then you won't have so much time to think only of you.

BELIEVE

Genesis 17:1-5, Romans 4:11, Galatians 3:22,

1 John 3:23

In the world people say seeing is believing; but in Christ, we know that you have to believe in order to see the goodness of God. Not see, then believe, the goodness of God; it is the faith that brings forth the seeing because we believe.

THE ORDER OF RESPECT

Honor, obey, and respect God;

Then respect yourself;

Then respect others,

And you will get respect.

WHEN WILL YOU LISTEN?

Jeremiah 17:5-7 Isaiah. 55:6-9

When will you listen to God? He'll tell you about people. You have trusted everybody and everything that you see, now try trusting the One you can't see: Jesus. He will set you free.

Learn God and stop listening to people.

RECEIVING THE BEST

The LORD gives you the best when you are at your best in representing Him.

THE MATTER

John 4:5-29, Matthew 9:1-25, John 11:1-46

Get your mind off the matter.

Focus the solution (Jesus).

The solution is the conclusion to the matter.

The Bible says that Jesus is the solution to the matter,

and all that chatter just don't matter.

DON'T OVERCLEAN

Matthew 23:25-26 1 Chornicles 22:19

Don't overclean the house and forget about the heart. The Lord is looking for a clean heart; not so much a clean house, but a heart that is truly seeking Him.

PURPOSE

God, You give us the necessities to live.

He wants us to give our time, talents, services, love, compassion, kindness, willingness, and money in order to help others.

YOU CAN'T LEARN IF

You can't learn if you don't listen.

You can't learn if you never try.

You can't learn if you never do.

You can't learn if you don't want to.

PERSONAL

Whatever you do should be a committed, contented covenant between you and God.

STOP TRIPPING

Stop tripping over yourself because you can't see anyone else.

Take a look and see who it is you're suppose to please; it can't possibly be you because here's what you should do.

Jesus wants us to do the same things He did for me and for you.

So stop tripping over yourself,

Before you look around and there's only you that's left.

ONLY ONE WAY

Psalm 18:30 John 14:6

Everybody is trying to do things their way,

Trying to keep God out of the way,

When Jesus is the only way.

GOD ISN'T LOST

Luke 15:11-32 Jeremiah 29:11-13

Looking for God? He isn't lost; we are.

Follow God; you can't get lost. He knows where we are concerning everything.

KNOWLEDGE BY GRACE

Knowing your Bible is the heart of wisdom for such a time, as this shaped by grace.

NO FEELINGS, NO COMPASSION

We have been putting stuff first before we put people first that we have become as cold as the stuff.

DON'T BE DISAPPOINTED

Each disappointment is a re-appointment that God is assigning you to something else.

YOU CARRY ME

Philippians 4:13

Lord, You pick me up when I'm down,

And You always change my frown.

You place my feet on solid ground,

And let me know You're always around.

You know I expect You to be there,

Because I know that You care.

You give me strength when I'm drained.

I know that is why You came.

DON'T MISS THE MESSAGE

Don't hear just the music, but make sure you hear the message. The music is to get your attention. The message is for you to pay attention.

TRUST JESUS' WILL, NOT ALWAYS A PILL

Psalm 30:2, James 5:14, Psalm 103:2-4

You feel the doctor gives pills, but Jesus always heals. Trust Jesus, not just the pill.

LEARN TO BE THANKFUL

1 Thessalonians 5:18, Psalm 107:1, Ephesians 5:20

We are always complaining,

But never thanking.

Jesus is the one who's doing the ranking, so why can't we just be thankful?

HOW TO GET GOD'S BEST

2 Chronicles 15:7, Galatians 6:9,10, Jeremiah 29:11

We get what we get, which is less than God's best because we don't appreciate what He has already given us: His son Jesus. Appreciate Jesus because He is the best.

FORGIVENESS

Matthew 6:14-15

Until you accept God's forgiveness,

Then forgive yourself, you cannot

Forgive anyone else. Do you know

God will not forgive you? God forgives over and over again. This is how you win over sin. We are not God; He's God alone. He is the one that sits on the throne.

WHEN THE MIND CHANGES THE HEART

Changes - Romans 12: 2, Ezekiel 36:26-27,

Psalm 119:11

God wants us to change our minds to think like Jesus, and our hearts to feel like His. If we change our way of thinking, then the heart will change.

EVIL MAN, NOT EVIL MONEY

Matthew 6: 21-24 1 Timothy 6:9, 10

Money is not the root of all evil; it is when the evil man chooses to love the money rather than God that the love of money becomes rooted in his soul. Then will consume him.

JESUS' LESSONS

Matthew 7: 13-14

Jesus wants us to learn all about life, not try to live the world's life;

so that we can have eternal life.

NEED PATIENCE,
JUST ASK

Matthew 7:7-8

If you don't have patience, and you desire to have patience, ask God. He said you have not because you ask amiss.

STOP LOOKING BACK

Stop looking back, and you will see.

That life you had is used to be.

You cannot keep helping yourself;

To stay in the past where there's nothing you've left.

God gives us and you a way of escape, and that's the road that

we should take.

His name is Jesus, and He is the way.

So please follow Him today.

Grab hold of Jesus, and don't turn

around so you can receive your crown.

THE TEST

When your test becomes a mess,

It is not God; it is the devil at his best. God doesn't
make messes.

He is always blessing.

WRONG THINKING

Isaiah 55:7-9

God gave us free will to think.

Don't let what you think control you.

Only what God says really matters.

RELIGIOUS NOTHING

Religion is nothing if there's not a heart for God in it.

DON'T MESS UP

Don't mess up what you have trying to hold onto what you had.

Let go of the past, so that you can see the present and move onto the future.

IT JUST WON'T WORK

Philippians 4:13

Things will not work right for you or us until we work it out with God.

DON'T LIMIT GOD

Psalm 78:37-42 Jeremiah 29:11

If God is not in it, there is a limit. When God is in it, there's no limit. Keep God in everything, and He will withhold no limits of blessings in your life.

SIN MUST EXIST

Isaiah 46:8-12

I have allowed sin since the beginning of time,

Just to show you who I am.

I could stop it, if I please;

But then you'd have no need for Me.

I will fix this in My time,

But in the meantime please don't whine. Pray.

JESUS CALLED US TO DIE

Jesus called us to die to self; not to serve self, but to live for Him;
And to serve others, then self. It makes Him happy; now we can be happy.

PAY ATTENTION

When you go to church and don't give God your attention, it's not that He can't get it.

But you should pay attention.

Oh, did I mention;

It's for your life extension.

FOLLOW THE
RIGHT PERSON

John 10:9-15

When you follow people, trouble comes.

When you follow Jesus, life comes;

And it will come more abundant.

Follow the cross (Jesus), not the crossroads (people).

Jesus will always be there,

But people come and go.

BELIEVE GOD'S WORDS

2 Timothy 2:15

If you don't believe it,

You won't receive it.

If you don't read it,

You won't know it.

If you don't know it,

You can't use it.

THANK, NOT COMPLAIN

Numbers 11:1-6, Philippians 2:13-15

If we do more thanking than complaining, and realize that God is doing the ranking, we would not get so many spankings. Let's thank God in everything and for everything.

BAD ADVICE vs. GOD'S PROMISES

Psalm 89:34, 1 Samuel 12:22, Joshua 1:5

We ask everyone in the world for advice, but it's only God who holds our lives.

He holds our lives in His hands, and it only works at His command.

So stop going to the world for advice, since He is the one that holds your life.

Don't hold onto the world's changing hand,

Because the Word of God will always stand.

Hold on to God, and He will hold you.

I AM GOD

I AM God, and God alone. I am the one that sits on the throne.

I sit high and I look low, and follow you wherever you go.

You can't hide from me anywhere; that is just how much I care.

So when you're ready to come to Me, please come to Me on your knees.

BE ABOUT GOD'S BUSINESS, BUT DON'T BE A BUSYBODY

2 Thessalonians 3:11, 1 Timothy 5:11-14, Peter 4:15

Let's not be so busy carrying our mouths and bodies from house to house to spread anything that doesn't concern us.

Let's spread the gospel, not the gossip.

ARE YOU OFFENDED OR ENCOURAGED?

OK

I GOT YOUR ATTENTION.

LET'S BELIEVE.

LET'S TALK.

LET'S WIN FOR CHRIST.